AF705833

SAFEGUARDS KNOWLEDGE MANAGEMENT ACTION PLAN

AUGUST 2025

ASIAN DEVELOPMENT BANK

ADB

6 ADB Avenue, Mandaluyong City, 1550 Metro Manila, Philippines
Tel +63 2 8632 4444; Fax +63 2 8636 2444
www.adb.org

ISBN 978-92-9277-383-0 (print); 978-92-9277-384-7 (PDF); 978-92-9277-385-4 (e-book)
Publication Stock No. SPR250304-2
DOI: http://dx.doi.org/10.22617/SPR250304-2

Note:
In this publication, "$" refers to United States dollars.

Cover design by Rocilyn Locsin Laccay.

Acknowledgments
This plan was prepared by ADB consultant Patrick Lambe of Straits Knowledge in collaboration with the policy and technical services team of the Office of Safeguards. Please direct questions to Lisa Kircher at lkircher@adb.org or Patrick Lambe at plambe@straitsknowledge.com.

Contents

Tables and Figures

TABLES

FIGURES

Abbreviations

ADB	Asian Development Bank
DMC	developing member country
DOCK	Department of Communications and Knowledge Management
ESF	Environmental and Social Framework
ESS	environmental and social standard
ISMS	Integrated Safeguards Management System
KM	knowledge management
KMAP	knowledge management action plan
NOM	new operating model
OSFG	Office of Safeguards

Foreword

The Safeguards Knowledge Management Action Plan (KMAP) is a strategic initiative by the Asian Development Bank (ADB) Office of Safeguards to improve knowledge management of safeguards. This plan aligns with ADB's Strategy 2030 and the broader bank-wide KMAP 2021–2025. It addresses the bank's transition to a new operating model and the rollout of the updated safeguard policy—the Environmental and Social Framework—effective in January 2026. The Safeguards KMAP aims to improve knowledge sharing, collaboration and the systematic organization of safeguards knowledge within ADB. The plan focuses on learning from experience, ensuring ongoing access to the knowledge of experienced staff, and sharing common knowledge resources that are easily accessible. It also emphasizes the importance of peer-driven, expert-informed learning processes to help implement the new policy framework and increase the effectiveness of safeguards in ADB projects.

Nianshan Zhang

Nianshan Zhang
Head, Office of Safeguards
Asian Development Bank

Executive Summary

To enable the Asian Development Bank (ADB) to effectively implement its safeguard function and policy, the Office of Safeguards (OSFG) is adopting a strategic and integrated approach to knowledge management (KM). The Safeguards Knowledge Management Action Plan (KMAP) aims to ensure KM interventions for safeguards

- align with Strategy 2030 and the ADB-wide KMAP,
- address changes related to the transition to a new operating model (NOM) and new safeguard policy rollout,
- tackle both existing and emerging needs and opportunities within the safeguards community, and
- support improved safeguards within ADB projects.

In this document, "knowledge" is defined by ADB as "information or understanding that enables action to create value through increased productivity and innovation." In this plan, the word refers to all forms in which knowledge can be used or shared within the organization to better perform its work. This includes documents, data, communications, established routines and systems, documented or undocumented effective ways of working, skills and competencies, experience, expertise, and tacit knowledge accumulated through institutional memory.

The term "knowledge management" refers to any management actions, processes, or activities that seek to improve

- access to knowledge,
- knowledge sharing and collaboration,
- organizing knowledge for reuse,
- synthesizing knowledge,
- communicating knowledge,
- learning, and
- knowledge acquisition.

This action plan is based on an analysis of current issues facing the ADB safeguard function, including the shift to the NOM and new policy—the Environmental and Social Framework (ESF)—and consultations with stakeholders held in August and November 2022 on knowledge-related issues and opportunities. The consultation sessions examined

- ADB KM roles, such as the Department of Communications and Knowledge Management (DOCK) staff and KM focals throughout the organization;
- safeguard roles in headquarters and resident mission field offices;
- portfolio managers' roles;
- safeguard roles for nonsovereign (private sector) operations; and
- existing safeguard KM initiatives, such as the Safeguards Community Site, the draft Safeguards KMAP, development of the Integrated Safeguards Management System (ISMS), the workforce requirement study for safeguards, and the need to develop an expertise locator.

Part 1 of this plan provides the context, rationale, and guiding framework for the Safeguards KMAP.

Part 2 summarizes the key findings of the KM needs analysis conducted in consultation with both safeguard and non-safeguard staff. It also discusses the implications of the findings in the context of the NOM and updated safeguard policy rollout.

Part 3 describes the vision, measurable outcomes, and implementation road map. It includes a capacity and resource plan to support the road map. These plans have not been updated since the Safeguards KMAP was approved and distributed within ADB in December 2023.

Safeguards Community Site
This knowledge portal for safeguard materials is housed within the internal ADB SharePoint system, accessible to staff, consultants, and contractors. This action plan includes a revamping of the current site to make it more useful and easier to navigate.

1 Context: Why a Safeguards Knowledge Management Action Plan?

There are three major drivers for a Safeguards Knowledge Management Action Plan (KMAP): the Asian Development Bank (ADB) KMAP, the new operating model (NOM), and the safeguard policy update to the Environmental and Social Framework (ESF).

ADB Knowledge Management Action Plan

ADB is more than halfway through the bank-wide 5-year ADB KMAP 2021–2025 to support its Strategy 2030 goals. As shown in Figure 1, knowledge management (KM) should support Strategy 2030 by

- enhancing collaboration and adopting a One ADB approach to increase learning, innovation, and impact on the bank's developing member countries (DMCs);[1]
- improving the quality of knowledge services; and
- using member-focused approaches and promoting lesson sharing and good practices among economies and regions.

Figure 1: Excerpt from the Asian Development Bank Knowledge Management Action Plan 2021–2025

A. Strategy 2030 and Knowledge Management

The Knowledge Management Action Plan (KMAP) 2021–2025 connects bank-wide reforms to improve how ADB manages knowledge in all its business processes to give effect to the knowledge provisions of the Asian Development Bank (ADB) Strategy 2030 (Box 1). Strategy 2030 is clear about how ADB should strengthen its knowledge services:

(i) Increase collaboration by instituting a "One ADB" approach, bringing together knowledge and expertise from across the organization to increase learning, innovation, and impact in developing member countries (DMCs).

(ii) Improve the quality of knowledge services through deeper analysis and research, expedite greater knowledge sharing across countries, and make business processes more efficient.

(iii) Use country-focused approaches, emphasizing practical knowledge that fits local conditions; identify lessons; and replicate good practices across the region and beyond.

Source: Asian Development Bank (ADB), KMAP.

[1] The One ADB approach is part of Strategy 2030 and is designed to bring together expertise and knowledge in a range of areas across the institution.

The ADB KMAP provides a framework for KM planning, and this Safeguards KMAP aligns with the framework as detailed in Section 3.

People and culture. To foster knowledge sharing and development, both internally and externally, by building capacity and expertise.

Processes and systems. To establish efficient processes and systems for sharing, capturing, and reusing knowledge within the flow of daily work.

Relationships. To overcome the limitations of knowledge silos and functional barriers and to strengthen networks and collaboration, both internally and externally.

In line with the ADB KMAP objectives, the Office of Safeguards (OSFG) has undertaken several initiatives to

- improve the Safeguards Community Site to facilitate knowledge-sharing and collaboration,
- streamline and digitize safeguard procedures and documentation through a new Integrated Safeguards Management System (ISMS),
- explore the application of behavioral science to improve implementation of safeguards, and
- implement a capacity-building program for ADB staff and DMCs.

Knowledge management implications. The ADB safeguard function is undergoing major changes and the OSFG is seizing this opportunity to adopt a more strategic approach to its KM needs, ensuring an integrated and systematic strategy. In conjunction with the major changes and requirements listed below, this Safeguards KMAP aims to ensure that ADB's KM interventions

- align with Strategy 2030 and the ADB KMAP;
- address changes related to the transition to a new operating model (NOM)[2] and new safeguard policy rollout;[3]
- tackle both existing and emerging needs and opportunities within the safeguard community; and
- support improved safeguards within ADB projects.

New Operating Model

ADB underwent a significant organizational restructuring known as "the new operating model" or NOM on 30 June 2023 to improve organizational effectiveness and empower staff to maximize development impact to fully achieve the objectives of the Strategy 2030. This includes a focus on developing holistic, knowledge-based, innovative, and integrated solutions, particularly by promoting a One ADB approach and improving the quality of knowledge services.

About 1,000 staff across ADB have new reporting structures, either as direct reports or through new matrix reporting. This restructuring aims to improve collaboration, consolidate technical knowledge, and facilitate more flexible deployment of technical knowledge.

As part of this reorganization, all safeguard staff at headquarters and in resident missions now report to the OSFG. Moreover, there has been significant new recruitment for safeguard roles.

Knowledge management implications. From a KM perspective, this implies the need for (i) more systematic knowledge sharing, reflection, and learning processes to optimize oversight, governance, and business process redesign; and (ii) improved onboarding and transition support, including information, networking, and team building during the steep learning curve throughout the bank-wide transition and change period.

[2] Footnote 1.

[3] The 2024 safeguard policy, called the Environmental and Social Framework (ESF), was approved by the ADB Board of Directors in November.

Safeguard Policy Update—The Environmental and Social Framework

The updated safeguard policy—the Environmental and Social Framework (ESF)—was approved in November 2024 and becomes effective on 1 January 2026. The ESF consists of ADB's policy vision statement, an environmental and social policy, and the following 10 environmental and social performance standards (ESSs) for borrowers and clients:

1. Assessment and management of environmental and social risks and impact
2. Labor and working conditions
3. Pollution prevention and resource efficiency
4. Health, safety, and security
5. Land acquisition and land use restrictions
6. Biodiversity and sustainable natural resources management
7. Indigenous Peoples
8. Cultural heritage
9. Climate change
10. Stakeholder engagement and information disclosure

Some of these standards relate to procedural knowledge and invite process improvement approaches (e.g., ESS 1 and ESS 10); some relate to well-established areas of practice (e.g., ESS 3 and ESS 4), while others are relatively new focus areas (e.g., ESS 2); and there may be marked regional variations in context. It is important to track the application of these standards across various contexts. Significant changes are also expected in the screening and risk classification process and guidance for safeguards in projects.

Knowledge Management Implications

Developing these standards and supporting guidance documents involves significant knowledge building and learning efforts. Implementing this new policy framework will also demand substantial learning and collaboration.

Consolidating all safeguard staff in one office requires substantial effort to establish a strong knowledge-sharing infrastructure and implement peer-driven and learning-informed processes to equip staff with the skills and information for their work and the support they need to adapt to the revised policy. A strong learning culture will benefit both staff in project implementation and future projects.

The learning processes are described as "peer-driven and expert-informed" for three reasons:

(i) OSFG requires rapid-cycle learning to provide staff access to field implementation experience to consider necessary adjustments to policy implementation and guidance. Peer-learning events are suited for this purpose, allowing for questions and shared experiences.

(ii) While the NOM aims to centralize and expedite access to technical knowledge and expertise, the revised policy rollout will increase the demand on experts' time. Peer-driven learning, supported by expert input and oversight, can alleviate routine consultation pressures on experts.

(iii) There will be an ongoing need to adapt, adjust, and interpret the new policy to accommodate local conditions, priorities, and needs. Robust processes are needed to blend local and technical knowledge to make policy decisions compliant with the relevant standards and suitable within the implementing DMC context.

2 Needs: Knowledge Management Gap Analysis

OSFG and Straits Knowledge held virtual stakeholder consultations from August to November 2022. These consultations included a structured survey on KM pain points in relation to safeguards, followed by emails and interviews to gather more contextual detail on the survey responses. They identified the strategic KM opportunities that facilitate implementation of the ADB safeguard policy. ADB Staff played an active role in the needs analysis with a 53% participation rate, and included the following stakeholders:

- staff with KM roles, such as DOCK staff and KM focals throughout the organization,
- safeguard staff in both headquarters and resident mission field offices,
- portfolio managers, and
- safeguard staff in sovereign and nonsovereign operations.

While consultations did not directly involve representatives from DMCs, the data collected reflects crucial internal stakeholder KM needs for DMC project development. Section 2.6 shows the knowledge flows and processes that benefit DMC interests, which serve as the basis for understanding and prioritizing KM needs.

The detailed findings from the consultations are documented in the report Safeguards Knowledge Management Needs Analysis submitted by Straits Knowledge in December 2022. Following the report's five focus areas for improvement, OSFG and Straits Knowledge conducted a second round of consultations in April and May 2023 to further investigate the community site, the ISMS, the development of a staff directory to locate in-house experts, and prior work on safeguard workforce requirements.

This section of the report summarizes the primary findings from the KM needs analysis and discusses the additional implications of the transition to the NOM and the revised policy.

The five focus areas are

(i) learning from experience, turning lessons into improved practice (all groups),
(ii) ensuring ongoing access to the knowledge of experienced staff (all groups),
(iii) sharing common knowledge resources (relevant for all, with lower priority for the East Asia Department, which was more focused on mutual alignment and coordination),
(iv) improving mutual alignment and coordination (all groups), and
(v) improving internal capacity building (a special concern for portfolio managers).

Focus Area 1: Learning from Experience, Turning Lessons into Improved Practice

The Safeguards Knowledge Management Needs Analysis Report 2022 Section 2.1 found that:

> *While there are ways to capture and document lessons, such as through project completion reports, these lessons are inconsistently applied across the safeguard and project implementation community. There is no systematic and consistent process for translating lessons captured into practice improvements. Additionally, there is no systematic provision for analyzing lessons from projects and identifying broad trends leading to systemic,*

policy, procedural, or guidance changes. Even when lessons are captured and documented, they are not readily available nor actively shared with other relevant teams in ADB. All respondent groups cited this issue as a major pain point.[4]

The transition to the NOM and the ESF underscores the importance of learning and broadens the scope of the challenge beyond improving the capture and reuse of project lessons to include the need for peer-led and expert-informed rapid-cycle learning, as described in Section 1.3.

Section 3 below describes how this learning culture can be embedded to ease the transition to the new policy and increase the effectiveness of implementing safeguards within projects.

Putting learning processes into practice that ease the transitions to the NOM and ESF is a quick win that can be achieved in this area. There is also ongoing work on identifying highly valuable lessons as case studies to support the ESF rollout.

Focus Area 2: Ensuring Ongoing Access to the Knowledge of Experienced Staff

The safeguard community comprises individuals with extensive experience, knowledge, and networks. This includes expertise on safeguards, technical knowledge, local knowledge covering legal and legislative approaches, mode of government operations, historical contexts, culturally appropriate ways of engagement, and skills in conflict resolution, consultation, and negotiation. Unfortunately, there are no systematic ways of passing on or retaining this knowledge, and the vulnerability of continued access to this knowledge when an individual leaves is often overlooked. Handovers are insufficient to address this challenge. Experienced individuals also maintain extensive personal records of past actions and decisions, and related discussions. Typically, only formal records are retained, and sometimes these are not even available to ADB, such as those produced by consultants, government partner agencies, executing agencies or implementing agencies. All stakeholder groups, except one department, cited this as a major risk.

This issue is associated with a lack of support for new hires or staff new to a role, who are often placed with minimal guidance or support. There are no systematic measures to support the learning curves of such staff. This concern was particularly noted by Central and West Asia Regional Department [sic] and SERD stakeholder groups.[5]

The transition to the NOM—which created OSFG—and significant increases in staff recruitment all underscore the need to enhance support for staff transition and onboarding. The KM needs analysis suggested that a designated team such as the safeguard policy team should cover the whole knowledge life cycle. This involves facilitating the learning curves of staff new to their role and helping staff build knowledge, skills, and expertise to alleviate the burden on the limited number of current safeguard experts.

While the development of an ADB expertise locator application may facilitate the discovery of relevant expertise when needed, the implementation of the ESF will likely intensify time demands on the limited pool of experts who will be called upon to address implementation and interpretation questions during the rollout of the new policy.[6]

Section 3 proposes several approaches to alleviate this burden by improving knowledge transfer and capture processes and providing support through a program of peer-led, expert-informed learning processes.

This area presents another opportunity for quick wins in KM if learning and support processes are established to facilitate staff transition to new working methods.

---

4 Safeguards Knowledge Management Needs Analysis Report 2022 Section 2.1.

5 Footnote 1.

6 The Economic Research and Development Impact Department of ADB has developed an internal expertise locator for staff to search for colleagues based on keywords reflecting geographies, sectors, or more specific expertise. The tool maps knowledge identified from publicly available ADB documents to individual staff and consultants.

Focus Area 3: Sharing Common Knowledge Resources

Policies, plans, and decisions lack thorough documentation, and when they are documented, they are often scattered and inconsistently organized, making them difficult to track down. There is an inadequate understanding of existing information resources, resulting in unnecessary duplication of work. People heavily rely on personal networks to get access to information, so if a key individual is unavailable, certain tasks become difficult to accomplish. Valuable knowledge resources may be possessed by individuals and when individuals leave, the knowledge is lost. ADB's previous structure led to safeguard knowledge resources generated in various places—OSFG, operations departments, resident missions—so it is crucial to gather and consolidate the materials.

Some of these issues are being addressed through the updated safeguard community site. However, more systematic issues persist around the inconsistency of filing systems and documentation processes across OSFG, resident missions, and the solutions group. Therefore, a two-pronged approach is required to (a) establishing a platform for shared knowledge, and (b) providing clearer guidance on governance for consistent documentation and filing processes. This ensures both that (i) safeguards-related knowledge can be searched and discovered across the community, and (ii) safeguard staff can easily navigate and contribute to consistent filing structures, regardless of their location.[7]

OSFG has made significant improvements to the Safeguards Community Site in SharePoint. It is now transitioning to a model of continuous, incremental improvements, with a focus on

- improving the quality, range, and usefulness of content;
- improving searchability and discoverability of safeguards-related content, both on the community site and elsewhere within the ADB ecosystem;
- simplifying collaboration, knowledge sharing, contribution, and reuse of previous interactions;
- integrating the new ISMS and OSFG hub site (internal site housing OSFG documents and information); and
- improving the ability to find past questions and experts' responses relevant to a user's current needs.

This shift to the NOM with new reporting lines and the development of the new ISMS present opportunities to introduce more consistent governance in recording and documenting work. Achieving more integrated information and data governance across the bank is also a top concern and current priority under the ADB KMAP. Therefore, any information governance initiatives within OSFG should be aligned with and support these broader initiatives.

Addressing the current dispersion of project documentation, inconsistency in documentation methods and processes for handover and takeover of project information pose substantial challenges. Consequently, while several immediate gains can be realized through ongoing improvements to the community site and ISMS rollout, the major benefits in this area will be medium-term and will vary once a new governance framework is developed and implemented. Section 3 describes how this can be achieved.

Focus Area 4: Improving Mutual Alignment and Coordination

Poor coordination within the safeguard community can lead to misalignment, conflicts, or errors because groups are unfamiliar with each other's plans and goals. Complex tasks that involve multiple teams can result in delays, errors, or quality problems. Consequently, external parties can exploit weak internal cooperation by seeking favorable opinions or playing one party against the other.

There is a need to build trust between safeguard staff, project teams, portfolio managers, and others. There is a perception that safeguard policy implementation primarily involves "policing" and "enforcement," at times relying on arbitrary judgments. From the safeguard perspective, there is a sense of having limited leverage and being low on project team

[7] Footnote 1.

priority lists. Safeguard staff can gain better reception by demonstrating willingness to listen to individuals with local knowledge, clearly explaining the reasons behind their decisions, and maintaining transparency without appearing overly assertive to the point of causing resistance or ill will.

Challenges include

- shifting mindsets from a perception of "policing" to facilitating project effectiveness and efficiency;
- establishing and communicating more objective decision criteria, maintaining consistency within a project, avoiding revisiting previous decisions or changing goals and addressing the perception of inconsistent policy understanding;
- balancing general ADB knowledge and safeguard requirements against context-specific knowledge and guidance; and
- ensuring that variations and exceptions based on local conditions do not become established as precedents for normal practice.[8]

Regarding this KM need, the shift to the NOM and the introduction of the ESF pose both opportunities and challenges, including:

(i) Establishing OSFG and developing a standards-based ESF should improve alignment, consistency, and coordination with colleagues across the safeguard community and with colleagues in projects and portfolio management.
(ii) The NOM impacts not only safeguard staff but also the way other staff access, use, and apply knowledge. Project teams are undergoing significant changes in their business processes and reporting lines. This can add pressure to project teams, making it more challenging to build mutual alignment and trust. However, it is also an opportunity to redefine the relationship between safeguard staff and other members of the One ADB project team, by using better-defined KM processes as a support mechanism.

This focus area has both infrastructure elements (e.g., creating a supportive knowledge base and a library of precedents for safeguard policy decisions) and capacity-building elements (e.g., building the skills of safeguard staff to navigate uncertainty and stress during a time of general transition). Section 3 will address both.

Focus Area 5: Improving Internal Capacity Building

There is a disconnect between the provision of training and the competencies required for safeguard work, where tasks are sometimes assigned to individuals without considering the skills required for the role. If competencies and skills for safeguard work are not systematically assessed during recruitment, staff development, and promotions, it can result in poor decision-making, poor guidance to clients, and, ultimately suboptimal projects.

This was a significant concern for portfolio managers. While not a primary concern for most respondents, the alignment issue (Section 2.4) also had a capacity-building component related to shifting the perception of safeguard work from being perceived as "policing" to being appreciated as a more collaborative, facilitative role.[9]

OSFG has conducted some work on analyzing workforce needs but has focused mainly on staffing levels and developing a staff directory with self-reported areas of expertise. There is still a need to systematically assess competency gaps, particularly in the context of the NOM. The preparatory work for a KM governance framework, as described in Section 3, will include a framework for a more systematic competency management approach. This area is linked to the previous focus area on improved alignment and coordination.

[8] Footnote 1.
[9] Footnote 1.

Critical Knowledge Flows for Developing Member Countries

Strategy 2030 and the ADB KMAP emphasize that DMCs are the ultimate beneficiaries of KM within ADB. The effectiveness of KM is measured by how much it benefits DMCs. Figure 2 illustrates the primary knowledge flows and knowledge activities that contribute to these benefits and shows the role of OSFG within these processes.

Figure 2: How Knowledge Management Within ADB Impacts Developing Member Countries and Private Sector Clients

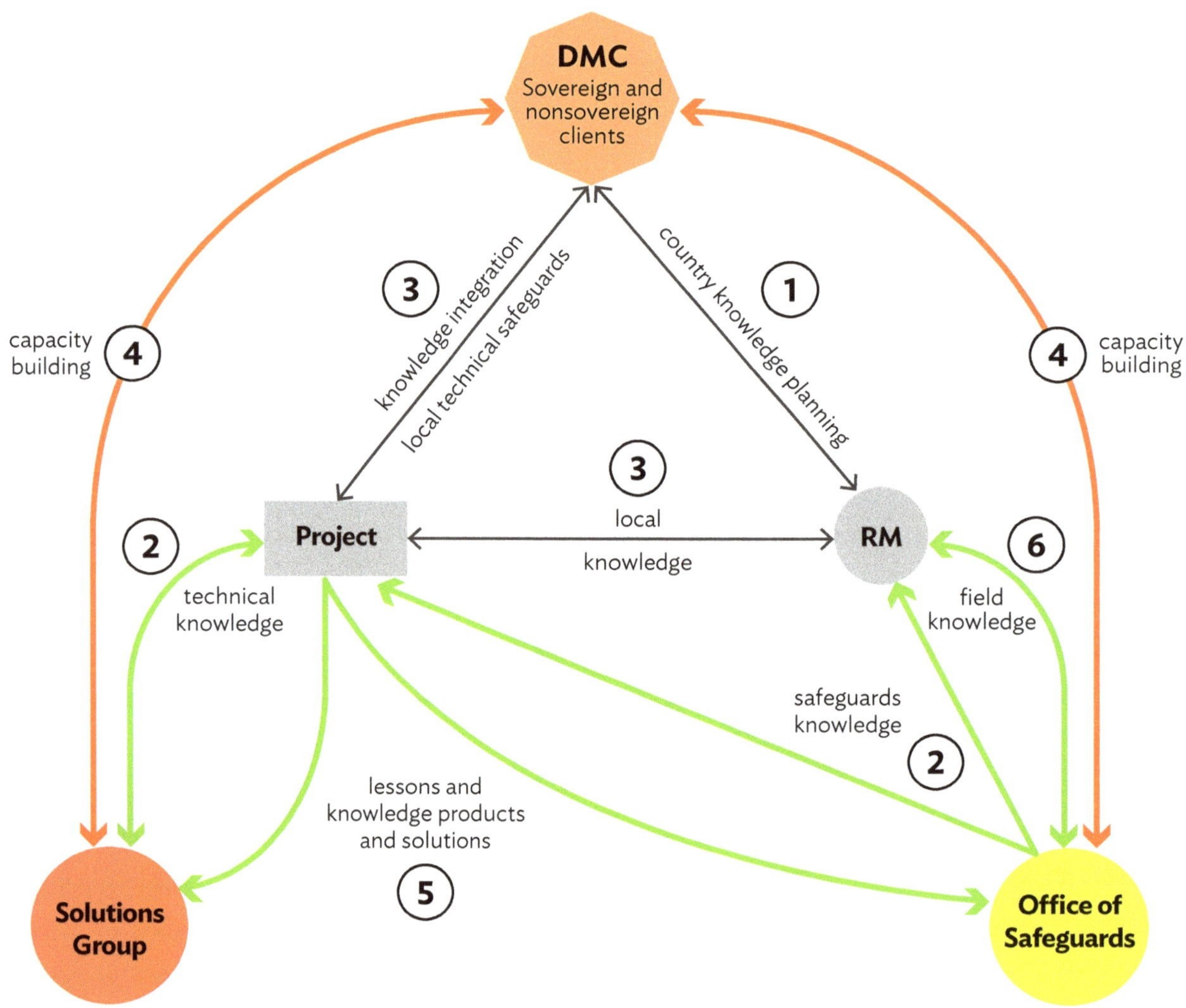

ADB = Asian Development Bank, DMC = developing member country, RM = resident mission.
Source: ADB Knowledge Management Action Plan.

The KM life cycle in relation to DMCs has six main phases.

(i) Through its resident missions, ADB develops a country knowledge plan with the partner government. It focuses on achieving knowledge outcomes aligned with the country partnership strategy to address development challenges. This sets the context for conceiving, framing, and developing projects in the DMC.

(ii) During project development, the Sectors Group provides technical expertise and knowledge to design and deliver sovereign and nonsovereign projects,[10] while OSFG works on risk assessments and mitigation measures to ensure the project is environmentally sustainable and socially inclusive. Figure 2 separates the knowledge flows from the Sectors Group and OSFG to highlight the safeguard knowledge element. Information flows among the Sectors Group, OSFG, and project teams must remain uninterrupted under the NOM.

(iii) From the KM perspective, close coordination in information and knowledge sharing needs assessment, gap analyses, and capacity planning among OSFG and project teams are crucial and should be closely monitored during the NOM implementation. Additional analysis may be necessary at the corporate level to understand and preserve effective knowledge flows among safeguard staff, project teams, and resident missions. Technical and safeguard expertise must be localized and contextualized to the conditions of the DMC. The resident mission plays an important role in developing and curating the local knowledge necessary to support this knowledge integration effort. Project teams and partner governments also need to develop knowledge integration processes to ensure that technical, safeguard, and local knowledge can be integrated effectively. Strengthening access to local knowledge may involve increasing national capacity, such as creating a pool of national consultants, and developing the capacity of national consultants where needed.

(iv) ADB may offer capacity-strengthening support to ensure project effectiveness in terms of technical implementation or safeguards. This includes provisions for continuity of knowledge within the DMCs as personnel changes.[11,12]

(v) ADB Staff learn and enrich their knowledge through field experience, expressed through lessons learned, project evaluations, knowledge products, and knowledge solutions.

(vi) The relationship between OSFG and the resident missions covers the flow of safeguard knowledge from OSFG to the resident mission and the reciprocal sharing of knowledge from resident missions to OSFG.

The Safeguards KMAP outlined below aims to support these critical knowledge flows and activities.

Summary of Knowledge Management Needs and Desired Outcome

The ADB KMAP is based on a theory of change that outlines expected outcomes and then explains the approach to achieving them. Figure 3 translates the results of the KM needs analysis into desired outcomes for both the safeguard community and ADB DMCs. These outcomes are based on the current situation analysis and the KM needs analysis conducted with stakeholders. They form the foundation for the four main workstreams of the Safeguards KMAP. When people work collaboratively, these workstreams contribute toward greater alignment and better coordination of safeguard activities within projects and to generally more effective implementation of safeguards within ADB projects. In turn, these result in improved development impact for DMCs. Section 3 outlines how these outcomes can be achieved.

10 "The Sectors Group is a single operational group comprising seven sector offices that aims to deliver sector strategy, initiatives, and integrated solutions that advance ADB's strategic agenda in the region with ADB clients." https://www.adb.org/who-we-are/organization

11 It is important to recognize that in complex areas such as safeguards or KM to support competencies and experience-building, capacity building takes time to achieve measurable impact. The Safeguards KMAP recognizes this by meeting capacity needs through both individual training interventions and providing for knowledge continuity and the development of shared knowledge through collaboration, sharing events, and deliberate knowledge transfer activities.

12 The Safeguards KMAP does not currently cover strengthening country safeguards systems, which would be a necessary part of implementing the new safeguard policy. The KMAP focuses first on building core internal KM capabilities.

Figure 3: Desired Outcomes for Safeguards Knowledge Management by Workstream

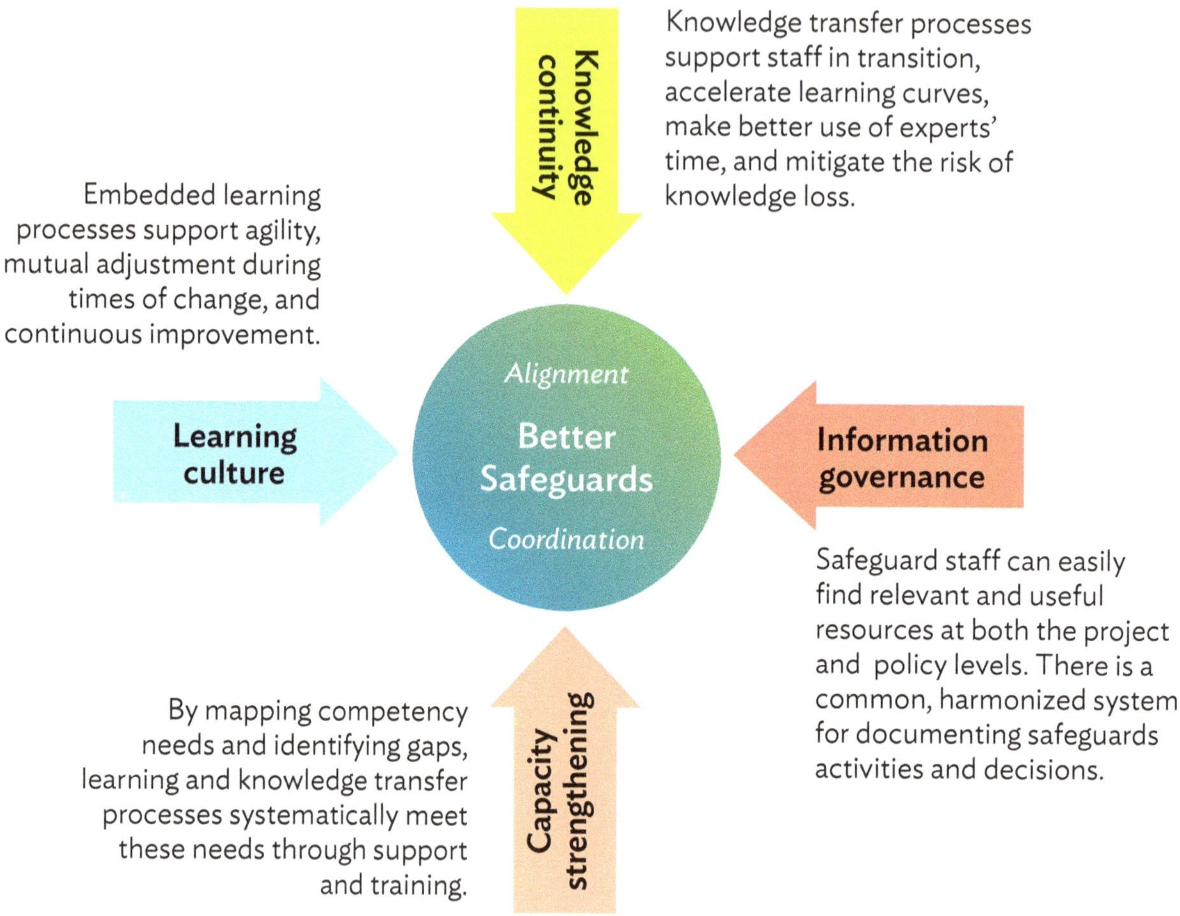

Source: Asian Development Bank.

This framework aligns with and reinforces the ADB corporate programs concerning KM.

Learning culture aligns with and contributes to ADB's Cultural Transformation Initiative.

Information governance aligns with ADB's overall KM governance activities, including the digital agenda, and work on the Electronic Documents and Records Management System and data governance.

Knowledge continuity aligns with the KM work in collaboration with sectors and themes, as well as on knowledge networks and communities of practice.

Capacity strengthening aligns with the country knowledge plan process.

3 Actions: Knowledge Management Action Plan 2024–2026

The suggested time frame for this action plan is 2024–2026 to address both immediate and medium-term needs, considering the evolving state of safeguard policy implementation. It includes a formal review and evaluation of the action plan with the ADB KMAP renewal process in 2025.

Knowledge Management Vision

The KM vision for safeguards is "to continuously improve our practices to deliver better safeguards."

The purpose of KM is to strengthen safeguard implementation in ADB projects for DMCs by

- ensuring project learning is translated into improved practices across the safeguard community;
- providing regular learning opportunities for less experienced staff to benefit from the knowledge of more experienced staff;
- providing easier access to the documented knowledge and data of the safeguard community, including a shared knowledge base, cross-site search, and other more consistent methods of documenting and reporting on project work;
- minimizing inconsistencies in the application of the safeguard policy within and across projects, through structured handover/takeover processes, access to precedent decisions, and access to clear documentation of the considerations behind decisions;[13] and
- ensuring that ADB Staff and DMC partners have access to the competencies, skills, and technical and local knowledge required for effective work in delivering high-impact projects with effective safeguard provisions.

Achieving the points above is expected to lead to the following measurable outcomes:

- improved overall effectiveness of safeguards in projects, assessed through evaluations and complaints, and KM contribution to this improvement;
- faster adaptation to new roles of staff new in a post,[14] reducing the risk of knowledge loss when key members leave, as measured through staff surveys and management of a knowledge risk register;[15]
- streamlined and well-informed safeguard decision-making process and less time spent seeking basic information and documentation;
- improved perceptions of key clients on the effectiveness of safeguard decisions and support within projects, gathered through surveys, interviews, or other inquiry methods; and
- increased confidence and reduced stress levels among safeguard staff, as measured through surveys.

---

13 While "inconsistencies" was a pain point identified in the needs analysis, different approaches to risk assessment and risk management are sometimes necessary because of the context. Perceived inconsistencies need to be accounted for so that the rationale for a different approach is understood. A precedents library is important in the context of the new risk-based approach to demonstrate how decisions were made to encourage others and provide support.

14 "Speed to effectiveness" may include (i) bringing less-experienced staff up to speed, (ii) "leveling up" staff transferring from a different area of work, and (iii) integrating the expertise of an externally recruited person into the bank's working processes.

15 A knowledge risk register is an inventory of key knowledge areas that are at risk of loss (e.g., if a key person leaves), together with mitigation measures. It can be used to track risk over time.

Key assumptions:

- The KMAP's effectiveness will be evaluated on (i) its contribution to both the effectiveness of the safeguard work; and (ii) its contribution to a smooth transition to the NOM and the ESF.[16] Section 3.6 describes the proposed governance and evaluation of the Safeguards KMAP.
- The KMAP supports the broader change management program for the transition to the NOM and ESF by offering knowledge and learning services. These include KM planning frameworks, methods, processes, systems, and activities. The Safeguards KMAP is integrated with OSFG's broader change management program.[17]
- ADB KM efforts with DMCs and private sector clients aim to apply knowledge work at multiple levels, including government officials, executing agencies, and implementing agencies, both in terms of staff and management.
- KM practices developed to strengthen OSFG should be adapted and extended to DMCs and private sector clients as needed.
- Quantitative and qualitative indicators may not directly measure the value of knowledge work but provide proxies for the value of such work. It is important to validate any perceived measure or trend by sampling and gathering illustrative examples of impact and effectiveness of KM contributions.

Theory of Change: Summary of Workstreams

The theory of change describes the desired outcomes and details how they will be realized. The desired outcomes for safeguards KM will be achieved through the four workstreams introduced in Section 2.7 and summarized below. The details are covered in Sections 3.3 (Road Map at a Glance) and Section 3.4 (Detailed Road Map).

Workstream 1	**Developing a learning culture will be accomplished in the Safeguards Knowledge Management Action Plan by**
Embedded learning processes support agility, mutual adjustment during times of change, and continuous improvement. **Learning culture**	• reviewing and developing a framework for consistent lesson gathering, application, and reuse across the safeguard community; • analyzing and applying lessons to create knowledge and learning products, processes, and activities that lead to improved practices; and • supporting the transition to the NOM and ESF through a program of network learning and sharing events, guided by an agenda based on current learning and knowledge needs in collaboration with the capacity strengthening workstream.

16 In the near term, KM will be an important mechanism to support rapid learning and new knowledge building during a period of transition. It is not a separate function to be evaluated apart from how it impacts the main safeguard work of ADB. KM is working when it supports and improves the effectiveness of safeguard work.

17 The Safeguards KMAP supports the ESF rollout and the NOM as well as the change management programs for both.

Workstream 2	**Information governance will be accomplished in the Safeguards KMAP by**
Information governance Safeguard staff can easily find relevant and useful resources at both the project and policy levels. There is a common, harmonized system for documenting safeguards activities and decisions.	• upgrading the Safeguards Community Site to improve search, findability, discoverability, and to support collaboration, sharing, and problem-solving; • conducting a knowledge mapping exercise to chart how documents are currently stored and organized across OSFG, identifying useful resources for sharing; and • implementing a content and data governance workstream to consistently document, monitor, and report safeguard processes across the community, facilitate content and data transfer, and effectively target critical knowledge and learning opportunities.

Workstream 3	**Knowledge continuity will be accomplished in the Safeguards KMAP by**
Knowledge continuity Knowledge transfer processes support staff in transition, accelerate learning curves, make better use of experts' time, and mitigate the risk of knowledge loss.	• conducting a knowledge-mapping exercise to chart areas of dependency on critical knowledge and expertise and any risks or gaps; • establishing a knowledge continuity framework, risk register, and mitigation plan to include support for knowledge continuity in DMCs and private sector clients; • implementing a knowledge transfer workstream to ensure continuous access to critical knowledge areas and effective use of experts' time; and • developing an onboarding and transition support program to accelerate effectiveness and build knowledge in newer staff and those transitioning to new roles, as well as in DMCs and private sector clients.

Workstream 4	**Strengthening capacity will be achieved in the Safeguards KMAP by**
By mapping competency needs and identifying gaps, learning and knowledge transfer processes systematically meet these needs through support and training. **Capacity strengthening**	• conducting a knowledge mapping exercise to chart competencies and skills against key safeguard activities and to identify gaps and needs for OSFG in the immediate term and potentially for DMCs; • establishing a competency management framework along with an annual learning and training plan; this plan should include provisions for meeting competency needs through the learning culture workstream and the knowledge continuity workstream; and • supporting the transition to the ESF by organizing a program of network learning and sharing events of different scales. These should be peer-led, expert-informed, and guided by a learning agenda based on current learning and knowledge needs. This effort will be coordinated jointly with the learning culture workstream.

DMC = developing member country, ESF = Environmental and Social Framework, NOM = new operating model, OSFG = Office of Safeguards.
Source: Asian Development Bank, Office of Safeguards.

Road Map at a Glance

Figure 4 summarizes the proposed 3-year KM safeguard road map. It shows dependencies and connections between key activities and is color-coded by the types of resources required. The detailed road map activities are laid out in Section 3.4, organized by the pillars of the ADB KMAP.

Figure 4: Road Map at a Glance

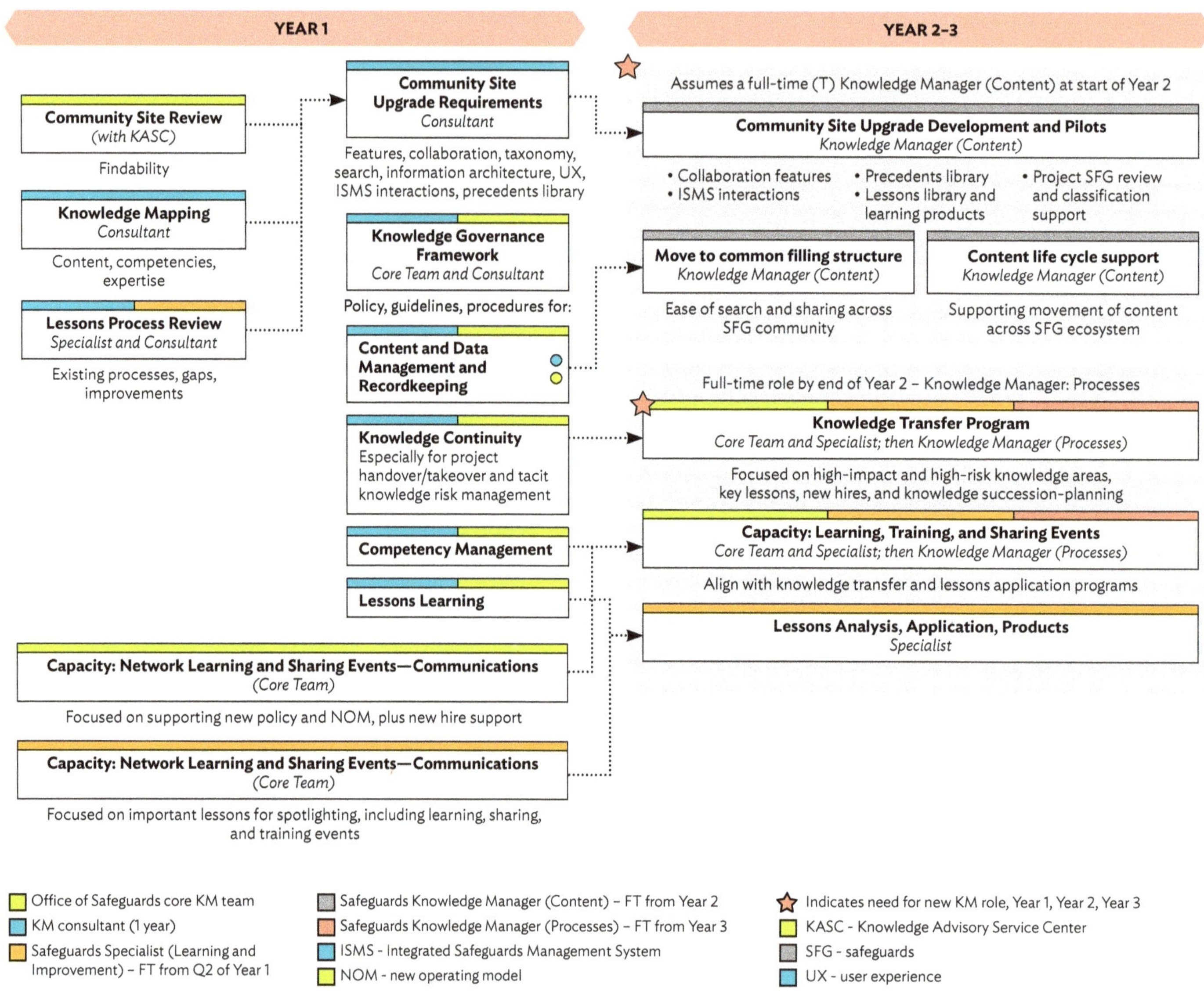

Source: Asian Development Bank, Office of Safeguards.

Detailed Road Map

Table 1: Detailed Road Map for Year 1 (2024)

People and Culture	Process and Systems	Relationships	Output	Resourcing
	Safeguards Community Site review with DOCK, focusing on search and findability		Safeguards Community Site v3 upgrade requirements covering collaboration, discussions, taxonomy, search, information architecture, content types/templates, ISMS interactions, precedents library, interactions with the expert locator • taxonomy and metadata framework	DOCK and search consultant
	Comprehensive knowledge mapping exercise focused on the ESF standards and processes, content and data sources and locations, competencies, competency gaps, expertise areas, and gaps or risks of loss Lessons process review of practices in lessons capture, documentation, access, and reuse across the safeguard community and through the lessons life cycle from projects to evaluations		Knowledge Governance Framework policy, procedures, guidelines for: • content and data management and recordkeeping • knowledge continuity, including handover/takeover for tacit knowledge and records; tacit knowledge risk management • competency management • lesson learning and lessons application	KM consultant Safeguards Specialist (Lessons Analyst) *new part-time role

continued on next page

Table 1 *continued*

People and Culture	Process and Systems	Relationships	Output	Resourcing
Plan and execute a learning and knowledge agenda for the year, including network learning and sharing events focused on addressing critical knowledge areas and providing peer support for adapting the ESF rollout (e.g., focused on ESF standards).[a] Formats for these events may include • safeguards learning sessions, knowledge markets or fairs, award ceremonies, peer team learning visits or study missions to critical or high-risk projects; • local applications such as training and sharing sessions; specific to DMC, region, sector, or theme and peer support for emerging challenges; • sharing sessions with other multilateral financing institutions; and • alerts and communications on new content, activities, and events. Develop an onboarding/transition support package for the first 3 months that includes key information resources, network-building activities, and regular check-ins			Knowledge base on ESF implementation, precedents library, reusable and searchable "ask an expert" Q&As by topic, peer review/ peer assist reports, learning and sharing mission reports, lessons knowledge base	Safeguard policy team and core KM team working with environmental and social standard leads[b] Safeguards KM team working with Safeguards Specialist (Lessons Analyst) *new part-time role
Lessons analysis and desk review leading to learning products and improved training or capacity-building events as well as knowledge content[c] Explore recognition or awards for project teams that contribute, for example, the • lesson with the greatest promise for impact on future projects, which can include informative failures as well as successes • best demonstrated implementation of an important lesson into a new project • best project for peer support			Learning and improving content and events • knowledge products, such as case studies • learning and training content • trends/emerging issues alerts • changes/improvements to policy guidance • award citations	Safeguards Specialist (Lessons Analyst) *new part-time role Safeguards KM team and ESF standards leads

DMC = developing member country, DOCK = DOCK = Department of Communications and Knowledge Management, ESF = Environmental and Social Framework, ISMS = Integrated Safeguards Management System, KM = knowledge management, Q&A = question and answer.

[a] The development of the learning and knowledge agenda may identify Technical Assistance (TA) requirements. This process needs to be synchronized with the operational and TA budgeting cycle (e.g., budget requests are due in August or September each year).

[b] The environmental and social standard leads are proposed here because they function like practice leads, harnessing and integrating knowledge from their various colleagues, partners, and stakeholders. This is a knowledge-intensive role, well suited to guide and shape the supporting knowledge resources and activities.

[c] These learning products are the outputs from the lessons analysis workstream and will provide additional input to feed into the shared knowledge base and into the learning and sharing events as appropriate.

Source: Asian Development Bank, Office of Safeguards.

Table 2: Detailed Road Map for Years 2–3 (2025–2026)

People and Culture	Process and Systems	Relationships	Output	Resourcing
	Safeguards Community Site upgrade (progressive rollout with pilots for different features), collaboration, discussions, taxonomy, search, information architecture, content types and templates, ISMS interactions, precedents library, interactions with the expertise locator, Q&A search and reuse, ESF knowledge base, lessons library, and learning content Year 3: Content migration of legacy content or content processing for findability through the community site		Improved findability and discoverability of common safeguard knowledge content Discoverability and access to documents within ISMS from within the Safeguards Community Site	Safeguards Knowledge Manager (Content) *new full-time role
	Implement consistent document and data governance across the wider safeguard network by • moving to a common filing system across OSFG; • implementing content life cycle management mechanisms to support portability and findability of content across the safeguard ecosystem (e.g., common templates, folder structures, common metadata/tags, handover/takeover procedures), which would be aligned with ISMS content life cycle management; and • improving the consistency of data gathering and management and better exploiting existing data to provide insights into the opportunities for improvement.		Maximize the ability to securely access, share, or discover documents and data across the safeguards community with minimum effort	Safeguards Knowledge Manager (Content) *new full-time role

continued on next page

Table 2 *continued*

<table>
<tr><th>People and Culture</th><th>Process and Systems</th><th>Relationships</th><th>Output</th><th>Resourcing</th></tr>
<tr><td colspan="3">Annually: Review, plan, and execute the learning and knowledge agenda for the year, covering network learning and sharing events focused on addressing critical knowledge areas and on providing peer support for adjusting to the ESF (e.g., focused around the ESSs). Formats may include
• safeguards community-wide knowledge markets, knowledge fairs, awards ceremonies, peer team learning visits, or study missions to critical or high-risk projects;
• local applications include training and sharing sessions specific to country, region, sector or theme, as well as peer support for emerging challenges within projects; and
• sharing sessions and collaborative activities and events with other multilateral development banks.

Years 2–3: Implement the knowledge continuity framework developed in Year 1 through
• deliberate knowledge building, transfer or capture activities for critical knowledge areas as well as at-risk tacit knowledge areas;
• including topics for sharing and learning on critical knowledge areas in the general program of learning and sharing events;
• succession planning for critical knowledge areas;
• implementing handover or takeover procedures for tacit knowledge and project-related documents and communications;
• extending the onboarding and transition support package to cover pairing of juniors with seniors on projects, as well as mentoring and coaching in soft skills, such as handling difficult conversations on projects and accounting for both power and gender differences; and
• developing improved handover and takeover procedures.

Year 2: Implement the competency management framework developed in Year 1, either folding competency building needs into the learning agenda for the year, or by providing training and e-learning that include a safeguard certification program.

Year 3 and annually: Review and update the competency management framework, identify current gaps, and adjust the training and learning plan.</td><td>Knowledge base on ESS implementation, precedents library, reusable and searchable “ask an expert” Q&As by topic, peer review/assist reports, learning and sharing mission reports, lessons knowledge base

Critical knowledge areas risk register and mitigation measures (reviewed annually)

Knowledge products and learning events based on knowledge capture events

Procedures for handover and takeover

Competency map and training and learning plan (reviewed annually)

Training and learning materials</td><td>KM core group transitioning by Year 3 to Safeguards Knowledge Manager (Processes)
*new full-time role

KM core group, transitioning by Year 3 to Safeguards Knowledge Manager (Processes)
*new full-time role</td></tr>
</table>

continued on next page

Table 2 *continued*

People and Culture	Process and Systems	Relationships	Output	Resourcing
Year 2: Continue the lessons analysis and desk review leading to learning products that feed into training, capacity-building events, and knowledge content. Incorporate the recommendations from the lessons application framework developed in Year 1. Year 2: Launch (e.g., at the annual retreat) recognition/awards for project teams that contribute • lesson with the greatest promise for impact on future projects (can include important failures as well as successes); • best demonstrated reuse of important prior lesson into a new project; and • best project-to-project peer assist. Year 3: Review and update the lessons application framework developed in Year 1			Learning and improving content and events Knowledge products (e.g., case studies) Learning and training content Trends and emerging issues alerts Changes or improvements to policy guidance Award citations Dashboard to monitor application and impact of key lessons from projects	Safeguards Specialist (Lessons Analyst) *new full-time role from Year 3

ESS = Environmental and Social Standards, ISMS = Integrated Safeguards Management System, KM = knowledge management, OSFG = Office of Safeguards, Q&A = question and answer.
Source: OSFG

Resourcing

The goal of the KM program is to significantly improve the effectiveness of safeguard work throughout the organization. This requires the dedicated time of a team of staff and consultants who have specialist skills, competencies, and experience for effective execution, including

(i) safeguard field experience, especially in analyzing and applying lessons learned;
(ii) expertise in content management, content governance, and search governance on a SharePoint/Microsoft 365 platform; and
(iii) proficiency in KM processes, methodologies, and facilitation.

The team will need to build on its detailed knowledge of how to support safeguard work and incrementally boost OSFG KM capacity over several years. Consistency, continuity, and specialized knowledge of KM and ADB's safeguard work are crucial. The KM program will require individuals with existing or developed deep contextual knowledge of safeguard work and will depend on strong networks across the community. The capacity of the team will grow in both substance and impact over time.

These needs will be considered and continually reviewed in the context of broader OSFG resourcing needs, and ADB's KM support for digital capability development.

In the past, there has been a heavy reliance on engaging consultants for specialized work such as knowledge management. The OSFG KMAP capacity and resourcing plan makes the case for provisioning more full time staff roles, for the following reasons:

- The goal of the KM program is to significantly improve the effectiveness of safeguard work throughout the organization. This requires the dedicated time of a team of specialist knowledge managers. While there will be immediate benefits, the program's full potential will be realized after a few years of sustained effort.
- This work requires both building on detailed knowledge of how to support safeguard work and incrementally boosting OSFG KM capacity over several years. Consistency, continuity, and specialized knowledge of KM and ADB's safeguard work are crucial.
- The KM program will require individuals with existing or developed deep contextual knowledge of safeguard work and will depend on strong networks across the community. All three new roles will grow in both substance and impact over time.
- Some aspects of the activities could be outsourced to consultants, and occasional external technical or advisory support may be required at points during the program. However, the more the roles and responsibilities are fragmented or outsourced, the less effective the overall KM program will become.

How This Knowledge Management Action Plan Should Be Governed and Managed

The Safeguards KMAP is intended to strengthen OSFG in its implementation of ADB's safeguard policy. It should focus on the most important knowledge and learning areas to increase OSFG's effectiveness and impact on DMCs. Therefore, the leadership of OSFG must direct and oversee it.

The leadership of OSFG should

- issue a clear statement of policy and expectations in support of the Safeguards KMAP once finalized;
- establish a regular reporting and review cycle, at least annually;
- provide input to the annual learning and knowledge agenda; and
- ensure sufficient resources are allotted to perform the tasks outlined in the plan, including assigning responsibilities under the KMAP and annual learning and knowledge agenda.

As Figure 2 illustrates, the Safeguards KMAP must be integrated with the bank's other KM activities, especially those involving DMCs. The Safeguards KMAP, as well as the annual reviews and updates to the KM activity plans, should include consultation with DOCK to

- ensure alignment with the ADB KMAP,
- optimize collaboration opportunities, and
- find synergies between safeguards KM and broader ADB KM initiatives.

The core KM team will undertake a coordinating, guiding, and advisory role to consultants and staff assigned KM tasks and be responsible for

- developing and updating performance indicators in line with the outcomes identified in Section 3.1;
- guiding KM communications across OSFG;
- evaluating and reporting on progress to the leadership of OSFG;
- organizing annual consultations across OSFG and key stakeholders on KM lessons learned, emerging KM and learning needs, and creating an annual learning and knowledge agenda with the help of KM staff and consultants; and
- initiating a KMAP review process at the beginning of Year 3, involving DOCK and OSFG leadership.

4 Conclusion

The Safeguards KMAP is an example of how useful it is to contextualize KM efforts for specific audiences and applications while remaining aligned with a broader organizational KM agenda. Using the ADB KMAP as a guiding framework, the Safeguards KMAP addresses OSFG's specific needs as it goes through an important transition and also leverages broader KM efforts.

The Safeguards KMAP

- brings focus and alignment to existing knowledge-related activities of OSFG, such as the regular "Tales from the Field" sharing sessions and the development of knowledge products;
- addresses the onboarding and competency development needs that come with an increase in staff numbers;
- supports internal and external capacity building with the development of the ESF; and
- has led to the incorporation of safeguards KM into the ADB-wide Digital Knowledge Management Project, with improvements planned for the use of SharePoint sites for knowledge access and sharing and the development of artificial intelligence-assisted tools to support safeguard work, both within OSFG and ADB-wide.

In all of this, the goal is to develop capabilities, practices, and systems that continuously improve the effectiveness of safeguard work across ADB.

www.ingramcontent.com/pod-product-compliance
Lightning Source LLC
Chambersburg PA
CBHW041800220926
51847CB00014B/271
* 9 7 8 9 2 9 2 7 7 3 8 3 0 *